Celebrate Passover

The Three Tables Haggadah
A Messianic Celebration

Joan Lipis

CELEBRATE PASSOVER
The Three Tables Haggadah
A Messianic Celebration

Original cover artwork by Betty Heinson, © 1988
Editorial services by Karen Roberts, RQuest, LLC
Interior formatting by Edie Glaser - www.craftingstones.com
Lamb illustrations by Natalie Cetti Groves

ISBN: 978-0-615-61070-2

Printed in USA

Contact the author at

web | www.novea.org
email | novea@novea.org

Novea Ministries
P.O. Box 62592
Colorado Springs, CO
USA 80962

Contents

Shalom

Congratulations! You've made a God pleasing decision to celebrate Jesus, accepting God's invitation to observe Passover for all generations. Although the command to celebrate Passover was first given to Israel, Passover, as all the Feasts of the Lord, belongs to the entire community of believers, both Jewish and Gentile.

Alfred Edersheim writes:

> When God bound up the future of all nations in the history of Abraham and his seed (Genesis 12:3), He made that history prophetic; and each event and every rite became, as it were, a bud, destined to open in blossom and ripen into fruit on that tree under the shadow of which all nations were to be gathered.[1]

Dr. Ron Allen describes Passover as "the fulcrum of the Old Testament as the Crucifixion is the apex of the New Testament." Passover is the most important event in Israel's history. The refrain of Passover echoes throughout Scripture.

While Passover has a unique significance to the Jewish people, its message of God's deliverance from bondage relates to the entire community of believers. We've all been delivered from the bondage to sin—sin that enslaves our bodies, our souls, and our spirits.

Bondage to sin keeps us doing things we don't want to do: bad ways of thinking, of talking, and of acting. Worst of all, bondage to sin keeps us separated from God's love and peace.

There are six important distinctives of Passover.

- Passover is celebrated in the month of Nissan, which begins God's calendar.

- Through Passover God revealed His memorial name.

- Passover begins Israel's history as a nation.

---

[1]   Edersheim, Alfred, *The Life and Times of Jesus the Messiah* (Grand Rapids, MI: Wm. B. Eerdmans Publishing, 1971), 210.

1

- The Passover event foreshadows God's ultimate redemption through Jesus the Messiah.

- Passover comes at the fullness of the month, at the full moon (as does the Feast of Tabernacles).

- Passover is an event and a season.

There are actually four feasts that relate to the Passover event: Passover, the Feast of Unleavened Bread, the Feast of Firstfruits, and the Feast of Tabernacles.[2]

THREE TABLES PASSOVER SEDER HAGGADAH

Seder means *order of service. Haggadah* comes from the Hebrew word [*maggid*] that means *to tell*. There are thousands of Passover Haggadot, but *The Three Tables Haggadah* differs from others in that it spans the entirety of God's redemptive plan. You start in Egypt, then go to Jerusalem and join Jesus and His disciples as they celebrate their last Passover together, and conclude with the Marriage Supper of the Lamb.

This *Haggadah* gives you the order of the Passover service and the liturgy that you need to conduct your Passover Seder. Seders require a bit of preparation, so I also direct you to our *Celebrate Jesus!* blog for simple but detailed instructions to help you conduct a Passover Seder in your home or church:

www.celebratejesusthebook.com/CJPassover

Over the years the Jewish people have added traditions and rituals to the celebration of Passover. I contend that it's more important to focus on the WHO we are celebrating rather than the HOW we celebrate. Therefore, the liturgy you now hold in your hand uses the rituals discerned from Scripture with the addition of only a *few* Jewish traditions.

Another difference in this liturgy is the emphasis on the participation of all guests and the use of co-facilitators. The Leader reads the traditional "father" role, and the Instructor provides the Christian perspective.

---

2   Passover commemorates the deliverance of Israel from the plague of death on the fourteenth day of Nissan. Unleavened Bread commemorates Israel's actual departure on the fifteenth day. Firstfruits is celebrated on the day following the Shabbat of Passover and commemorates Israel's entry into the Promised Land. Tabernacles is celebrated on the fifteenth day of the seventh month and commemorates the journey.

The Passover dinner should not be rushed; allow singing and a variety of discussions. Do not be bound to this liturgy. Instead, use it as a springboard to develop your own traditions. I have provided a suggested way for you to abbreviate the service. You may choose to omit the passages indicated with an [*].

Further notes can be found at the back of this book in a section titled Supplemental Notes and Explanation of Terms.

Scripture locations are deliberately not provided in the text of this Haggadah. It is to be used as a liturgical service, and the insertions of Scripture notations would be distracting. Also, quotation marks to denote word-for-word Scripture passages have, in most cases, been omitted for the same reason. A complete list of all Scriptures used, along with their locations, may be obtained by contacting the author.

My hope and prayer is that your love for Jesus will grow as you celebrate Him, our Passover Lamb!

Order of Service

Introduction

BEDIKAT CHAMETZ: SEARCHING FOR LEAVEN

For shorter services, omit paragraphs with [*].

LEADER: God commanded that every house be cleansed. Nothing made with yeast could be found if Passover was to be celebrated.

INSTRUCTOR: Leaven symbolizes sin throughout Scripture. As every animal to be sacrificed had to be without blemish, every grain offering (except on the Feast of Pentecost) had to be made without leaven.

*INSTRUCTOR: The Bible says: "All have sinned and fall short of the glory of God. If we claim to be without sin, we deceive ourselves and the truth is not in us."

*MEN: Surely the arm of the LORD is not too short to save, nor His ear too dull to hear. But your iniquities have separated you from your God; your sins have hidden His face from you, so that He will not hear.

*WOMEN: But if we confess our sins, He is faithful and just to forgive us our sins and to cleanse us from all unrighteousness. If we say that we have not sinned, we make Him a liar and His word is not in us.

LEADER: We have made a search of the house and every remaining bit of leaven has been burned. We can declare the house is ready to celebrate Passover. Now let us search ourselves for any leaven, for any impurity of thought, word, or deed that might separate us from the presence and the peace of God. Let us present our bodies as living sacrifices, laying aside every sin and weight that so easily ensnares us.

ALL (silently): O Lᴏʀᴅ, You have searched me and You know me. Before a word is on my tongue, You know it completely. Search me, O God, and know my heart; test me and know my anxious thoughts. See if there is any offensive way in me that needs to be removed as the leaven was removed from the house. Lead me in Your everlasting way.

(out loud): Let the words of my mouth and the meditation of my heart be acceptable in Your sight, O Lᴏʀᴅ, my Rock and my Redeemer.

LEADER: O God, we proclaim that You alone are God. You are the source of all we are and all we have.

ALL: In You we live and breathe and have our being.

INSTRUCTOR: We have set this night apart to remember Your mighty acts as You delivered us from bondage in Egypt and from sin. Through Jesus, Yeshua the Messiah, You redeem all who believe in You.

LEADER: O give thanks to the Lᴏʀᴅ, for He is good.

*ALL: His mercy endures forever.

*WOMEN: Who remembered us in our need.

*MEN: And rescued us from our enemies.

ALL: For His love endures forever.

Bɪʀᴋᴀᴛ ʜᴀNᴇʀ: Lɪɢʜᴛɪɴɢ ᴛʜᴇ Cᴀɴᴅʟᴇs

INSTRUCTOR: These candles remind us that God enlightens our darkness. Their light reminds us of the words of Jesus: "I am the Light of the world. He who follows Me shall not walk in darkness, but have the light of life." Sadly many people still prefer to walk in the darkness of their ignorance, hatred, and pain.

☛ **All hostesses rise and light their table candles.**

HOSTESSES: May these holiday lights inspire us to use our gifts to spread Your word and light into all the world.

Baruah atah Adonai, Elohaynu Melech ha-olam, asher kideshanu be-Yeshua, or ha-olam asher bishmo anu m'adlikim ner shel yom tov.

ALL: Blessed are you O Lord our God, King of the Universe, who has sanctified us in Yeshua, the light of the world, in whose name we light the candle of the holiday.

☛ **Hostesses sit.**

KADDESH: THE CUP OF SANCTIFICATION

LEADER: During the meal we will drink four cups (glasses) of wine. Each cup remembers one of God's promises to Moses.

"Say to the people of Israel: 'I am the LORD;
I will **bring you** out from under the burdens of the Egyptians,
I will **rescue you** from their bondage, and
I will **redeem you** with an outstretched arm and with great judgments.
I will **take you** as My people, and I will be your God.'"

The first cup, The Cup of Sanctification, is based on the first of God's promises:

I am the LORD; I will **bring you** out
from under the burdens
of the Egyptians.

הוצאתי - hotzeti

8

INSTRUCTOR: *Kaddesh* comes from the Hebrew root [*qdsh*] meaning *holy*. *Sanctify* means to separate for holy service. God brought Israel out of Egypt to sanctify her for His service.

LEADER: God made a covenant with our fathers, Abraham, Isaac, and Jacob. He promised that from them He would make a great nation, a nation that would bless the world. So God separated the nation of Israel from all the other nations of the world.

INSTRUCTOR: Then God made a new and better covenant with His people—both Jews and Gentiles. It was a law not written in stone but written on our hearts through faith in Jesus. It is by faith in Jesus that we are sanctified and separated to live holy lives. Jesus said we are to be *in* the world, but not *of* it.

> ☞ **All raise the cup.**

LEADER: Let us take this first cup and proclaim together the holiness of this Passover holiday and remember that God has called us out of Egypt to worship Him in the beauty of holiness.

Baruch atah Adonai, Elohaynu Melech ha-olam, boray p'ree hagefen.

ALL: Blessed are You, O Lord, our God, King of the universe, who makes the fruit of the vine and has grafted us into the vine.

> ☞ **All recline to the left and drink.**

URCHATZ: WASHING THE HANDS

LEADER: Let us wash our hands before dipping food into any liquid.

> ☞ **Symbolically wash hands.**

KARPAS: EATING THE GREENS

☞ Table hosts distribute greens to all who then dip them into the salt water as the leader reads.

LEADER: The wine we drank was red in color, reminding us of the blood of the Passover sacrifice. These greens remind us of the hyssop that we used to apply the blood to the doors of our homes. We dip the greens into the salt water to remember our tears while in bondage.

☞ All eat the greens.

YACHATZ: BREAKING & HIDING THE MIDDLE MATZAH

☞ Leader and table hosts pick up the matzah bag.

LEADER: This is the Bread of Affliction, reminding us how we suffered in Egypt.

INSTRUCTOR: Notice that there are three compartments. The bag is called the *echad*. Echad is the Hebrew word that means one, but is a compound, a unity of several. This is the same Hebrew word used to describe one day (evening and morning) and one flesh (man and woman). It is the same word in Deuteronomy 6:4: "The Lord our God is one."

☞ Leader takes the middle matzah and breaks it. Leader then puts one piece back into the echad, wraps the other piece in an extra cloth, and hides it. This can be done by every table host at every table.

INSTRUCTOR: We too have eaten of the bread of affliction as a result of our own sins and the sins of others. It is sin, not God, that brings pain and suffering to the world.

The broken matzah reminds us of the affliction suffered by Jesus. The prophet Isaiah said: "In all our afflictions He was afflicted, and the Angel of His Presence saved them. He was wounded for our transgressions, He was bruised for our iniquities; the chastisement that brings us peace was upon Him."

The matzah also reminds us of the words of Jesus: "The bread of God is He who comes down from heaven and gives life to the world. I am the Bread of Life. He who comes to Me shall never hunger."

LEADER: We give thanks to You, O Lord our God, who caused us to hunger that we might know that man does not live by bread alone, but by every word that comes out of the mouth of God.

*****ALL**: Bless the Lord who daily loads us with blessings. Great is His faithfulness!

INSTRUCTOR: The Passover Seder is designed so that we remember and also experience what happened in Egypt on that first Passover. Let's pretend we are actually sitting with Moses and his family.

11

The Table of Moses

MAGGID: TELLING THE STORY

LEADER: God commanded that we remember this night for all generations because when we forget the goodness of God, our hearts wander far from Him.

MEN: God said, "When your children say to you, 'What do you mean by this service?' you shall say,

WOMEN: "This is the Passover sacrifice of the Lord, who passed over the houses of the children of Israel.'"

LEADER: These elements will help us tell the story.

☞ **Leader picks up and replaces the Seder plate.**

PESACH: THE PASSOVER

☞ **Leader and table hosts pick up and put down the bone.**

LEADER: We killed our lamb on the doorstep and, as a sign of our faith in God, put its blood

on the top and the sides of our door. The sign of the blood will protect us from the plague of death.

INSTRUCTOR: The blood, on the top, bottom, and each side of the door, made the sign of the cross! Jesus is the ultimate Passover Lamb. When we, by faith, apply His blood to our hearts, it is a sign and witness that we have been saved from the power and penalty of sin and death.

RACHTZAH: WASHING THE HANDS

LEADER: Once again we must wash our hands before eating food, but since it is Passover, only the master does so.

☞ **Leader and table hosts symbolically wash their hands.**

MATZAH: THE UNLEAVENED BREAD

☞ **Leader and all table hosts pick up and put down the echad.**

LEADER: This is the bread of our sorrow and affliction. It is made without leaven because there is no time for the bread to rise.

INSTRUCTOR: Jesus was sinless; there was no spot or blemish in Him. Though He was tempted as all men are, He did not sin. He is the Bread of Life.

MAROR: THE BITTER HERBS

☞ Leader and all table hosts pick up the horseradish.

LEADER: This is *maror*, or bitter herbs. It reminds us of the bitterness of our slavery.

INSTRUCTOR: Bondage to sin is the worst slavery of all.

KORECH: THE CHAROSETH SANDWICH

☞ Reader #1 picks up or points to the apple/nut mixture.

READER #1: This is *charoseth*. It looks like the mortar we used to make the bricks, yet it tastes sweet because of the sweetness of our deliverance.

☞ Reader #2 picks up and puts down cup of wine.

READER #2: The wine reminds us of the blood and of the joy of our salvation.

☞ Leader and all table hosts pick up the echad.

LEADER: Today we eat the bread of sorrow. We give You thanks that though weeping might endure for a night, joy comes in the morning.

☞ Using the matzah from the echad, table hosts give everyone a palm-sized piece of matzah. Use more if needed.

LEADER: *Baruch atah Adonai, Elohaynu Melech ha'olam, ha'motzee lechem min ha-aretz.*

ALL: Blessed are You, O Lᴏʀᴅ our God, who brings forth bread from the earth.

> ☞ **All eat a piece of the matzah.**
> ☞ **Table hosts distribute the bitter herbs.**

LEADER: We eat these bitter herbs so we never forget the bitterness of our slavery.

> ☞ **All dip a piece of matzah into the bitter herbs and eat.**

LEADER: We eat the bitter herbs and the charoseth together to remember the sweetness of our freedom.

> ☞ **Everyone makes a matzah sandwich of the bitter herbs and apple/nut mixture.**

LEADER: Thank You, O Lᴏʀᴅ our God, our Deliverer, our Redeemer, and our Savior.

Baruch atah Adonai, Elohaynu Melech ha'olam. Todah l'Yeshuatanu.

ALL: Blessed are You, O Lᴏʀᴅ our God, King of the universe. Thank You for our salvation.

> ☞ **All eat.**

LEADER: To help us tell the story, the youngest child asks four questions.

CHILD: Why is this night different from all other nights?

1. On every other night we eat leavened or unleavened bread. Why on this night only unleavened bread?

2. On every other night we eat any kind of vegetable. Why on this night only maror, bitter herbs?

3. On every other night we are not required to dip our vegetables even once. Why on this night do we dip twice?

4. On every other night we eat sitting or reclining. Why on this night only reclining?

INSTRUCTOR: The answers have significance to our lives as believers in Jesus.

1. The unleavened bread reminds us of Messiah's swift return, which will be "as a thief in the night." We continue to purge all leaven from our hearts so that we don't "shrink back" at His coming.

2. The bitter herbs remind us of our bondage to sin and to death, from which Jesus freed us!

3. As we dip the greens, we remember that Jesus promised to dry all our tears; and even now He turns our mourning into dancing.

4. We recline because Jesus has made us a kingdom of priests to serve our God by worshipping Him forever.

ARBAA BANIM: THE FOUR SONS

LEADER: Four times the Torah says, "You shall tell your children on that day…" From this comes the tradition of "The Four Sons" representing different attitudes to God.

*INSTRUCTOR: These sons have the same attitudes of many people today who still ask: "Why do you do this? Why do you believe this?"

LEADER: The wise son asks, "What is the meaning of God's commandments?"

ALL: It is the wise man who fears God and keeps His covenant.

LEADER: The wicked son asks, "What does this service mean *to you*?" By the way, he says, "*to you*" he is not considering himself as part of the community.

ALL: The fool says in his heart, "There is no God." Salvation is far from the wicked.

LEADER: The innocent son asks, "What does this mean?"

ALL: He is not set in his ways and needs to hear the wonderful story of God's power and goodness.

INSTRUCTOR: The simple son does not know what to ask. This son must be told clearly and carefully how the LORD God has brought deliverance to Israel in the past and to us all in the present. Invite him to accept God's offer of salvation.

LEADER: Our story actually began with Abraham, who lived in Ur, a city in Mesopotamia. Ur was a great city, a cultured city even by modern standards. The Chaldeans worshipped many gods and idols. Yet it was there that God spoke to a man named Abram (later to be called Abraham) and said:

"Get out of your country, from your family and from your father's house, to a land that I will show you. I will make you a great nation; I will bless you and make your name great; and you shall be a blessing. I will bless those who bless you, and I will curse him who curses you; and in you all the families of the earth shall be blessed."

READER #1: By faith, Abram left as the LORD had told him, and he traveled to Canaan. Later God made those same promises to Abraham's son Isaac and then to Isaac's son Jacob. Jacob became the father of twelve sons who became the princes of Israel.

READER #2: Eventually there was a famine in the land, and Jacob and his sons went down to Egypt to dwell. The stay was meant to be temporary, but it lasted over 400 years. At first Israel was treated royally because of Joseph, one of Jacob's sons who was already in Egypt and became master to Pharaoh's household. Life was good…for a while.

READER #3: But then a new king who did not know about Joseph rose to power. Instead of respecting Israel, this king was afraid because of our growing numbers and prosperity. He declared:

17

WOMEN: "Come, let us deal shrewdly with them, lest they multiply, and it happen, in the event of war, that they also join our enemies and fight against us, and so go up out of the land."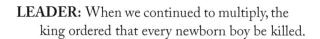

MEN: Therefore they set taskmasters over us to afflict us with their burdens.

LEADER: When we continued to multiply, the king ordered that every newborn boy be killed.

READER #4: Despite our misery, we had hope. We remembered the stories our fathers had told us about God. We didn't know too much about Him, but we remembered the promises He had made to Abraham, Isaac, and Jacob. So we cried out to Him.

MEN: God **heard** our groaning, and God **remembered** His covenant with Abraham, with Isaac, and with Jacob. And God **looked** upon the children of Israel, and God **acknowledged** us.

WOMEN: The LORD said, "I have surely seen the oppression of My people who are in Egypt, and have heard their cry because of their taskmasters, for I know their sorrows.

ALL: "So I have come down to deliver them out of the hand of the Egyptians, and to bring them up from that land to a good and large land."

INSTRUCTOR: Abraham knew God as El Shaddai, but God gave to Moses His memorial name, the name by which He wants to be known: YHWH, the One who is intimately and actively involved in our lives.

If we hear the words of the Bible as a symphony, this is the refrain:

Man is in trouble and cries out to God, and God hears even a groan. God remembers His promises to us. God sees us, and He understands. Then God acts to help His people by coming down to deliver them.

Isn't that what God did for you too? For God so loved the world that He sent His only Son, Christ Jesus, who being in the form of God, did not consider it robbery to be equal with God, but made Himself of no reputation, taking the form of a servant, and coming in the likeness of men. And being found in appearance as a man, He humbled himself and became obedient to the point of death, even the death of the cross.

In God's perfect time, One greater than Moses, manna, or the Temple came down to deliver His people. The Hebrew word for *acknowledge* is [*yada*], meaning *to know by personal experience*. Because God lived as a man, there is nothing that you are going through that He does not understand.

☞ **Sing a worship song.**

Kos Hitzalti: The Cup of Deliverance

LEADER: We come to the second cup, the Cup of Deliverance, based on God's second promise:

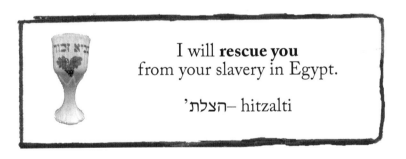

I will **rescue you** from your slavery in Egypt.

הצלתי– hitzalti

INSTRUCTOR: There are many Hebrew words for *deliver* and *rescue*. Here God uses the root [*ntsl*], meaning *a violent snatching away*. The word sounds like two pieces of Velcro being torn apart. The Cup of Deliverance reminds us of the violent way God snatched the Jewish people out of slavery, the same way He tore us from the grip of Satan.

Ester Hamakot: **The Plagues**

INSTRUCTOR: God demonstrated His love, His mercy, and His compassion by rescuing Israel from bondage. But this is only one side of His character. The Passover event reveals another side of God's character—His holiness, His power, and His justice. While God loves us, He must punish sin, especially the sin of unbelief.

LEADER: God had a message for Pharaoh:

ALL: "Let My people go that they might serve Me."

LEADER: But Pharaoh said, "NO!" He said, "Who is YHWH that I should obey His voice to let Israel go? I do not know YHWH, nor will I let Israel go."

INSTRUCTOR: Like so many today, Pharaoh had his own gods; he had his own way to worship. So God decided to show Pharaoh His power over the so-called gods of Egypt. Only God is God.

LEADER: God had warned Pharaoh that not believing in Him would mean trouble, but Pharaoh was too stubborn; his heart was too hard. Because of Pharaoh, everyone suffered as God brought nine terrible plagues on Egypt, each one worse than the one before. The plagues brought great destruction and sadness; yet if Pharaoh had chosen to believe, the plagues would have stopped.

INSTRUCTOR: The choice was Pharaoh's. But Pharaoh ignored God's warning that not believing in Him would result in death. God is holy; He cannot and will not tolerate sin. Sin must be punished. The one who sins MUST die.

LEADER: As we remember the first nine plagues, we also want to remember the pain Pharaoh inflicted on the people and on the land because of his choice.

> ☞ **As each plague is recited, drop a bit of wine from your glass onto your plate.**

All: Blood ~ Frogs ~ Lice ~ Flies ~ Disease ~ Boils ~ Hail ~ Locusts ~ Darkness

> ☞ **Leader invites people to suggest modern day plagues, such as cancer, war, drugs, etc.**

LEADER: The people suffered, the animals died, and the land was devastated. But still Pharaoh wouldn't change his mind. So the tenth plague would be the worst of all: death.

ALL: DEATH OF THE FIRSTBORN!

LEADER: God said, "I will pass through the land of Egypt on that night, and will strike all the firstborn in the land of Egypt, both man and beast; and against all the gods of Egypt I will execute judgment; I am the LORD."

READER #1: But God's love always provides a way of safety. God said, "On the tenth day of this month each family must choose a lamb or a young goat for a sacrifice. The animal you select must be a one-year-old male, with no defects.

READER #2: "Take special care of this chosen animal until the evening of the fourteenth day of this first month. Then the whole community of Israel must kill their lamb or young goat at twilight.

READER #3: "They are to take some of the blood and smear it on the sides and top of the door-frames of the houses where they eat the animal. That same night they must roast the meat over a fire and eat it along with bitter salad greens and bread made without yeast. Burn whatever is not eaten before morning.

READER #4: "Be fully dressed, wear your sandals, and carry your walking stick in your hand. Eat the meal with urgency, for this is the LORD's Passover.

ALL: "But the blood on your door posts will serve as a sign, marking the houses where you are staying. When I see the blood, I will *pass over* you. This plague of death will not touch you when I strike the land of Egypt."

LEADER: So as we sit here protected under the blood, the Angel of Death is passing throughout Egypt bringing death to the firstborn of Egypt—both man and beast. Every animal and every man that is firstborn is dying. This is God's justice.

INSTRUCTOR: Never forget that God had given Pharaoh a choice. We have the same choice: life or death. Giving us a choice is proof of God's love.

Let's try to imagine what it was like in Goshen that night. Pretend you are at the table of Moses. What do you hear? Is it quiet? Do you hear the cries of Egyptian people? Or do you hear the songs of praise coming from Jewish homes? How do you feel? Are you afraid, or do you trust God? You've seen how He has protected you all. You have been safe under the shadow of His wings.

MEN: The name of the LORD is a strong tower.

WOMEN: The righteous run into it.

ALL: And they are safe.

INSTRUCTOR: The LORD is a stronghold, "a wall of fortresses" to give refuge to all who will come under the shadow of His wings.

LEADER: Then God brought out of Egypt all who would believe in Him, both Jews and Gentiles. As a final show of His power, He parted the waters of the Red Sea so that Israel walked on dry ground. But on Pharaoh and his army, the waters came back, drowning them all.

> ↪ **All raise the Cup of Deliverance.**

Let us drink of the Cup of Deliverance with joy and thanksgiving.

Barruch atah Adonai, Elohanu Melech ha-olam boray p'ree hagefen.

ALL: Blessed are You, O Lord our God, King of the Universe, who makes the fruit of the vine.

LEADER: We will sing to You, O Lord, for You have triumphed gloriously! The horse and rider You have thrown into the sea! You, O Lord, are our strength and our song, and You have become our salvation. Your right hand, O Lord, has become glorious in power; Your right hand, O Lord, has dashed the enemy in pieces. And in the greatness of Your excellence, You have overthrown those who rose against You. Hallelujah!

☞ **All sing "Dayenu" on next page.**

Dayenu: It Would Have Been Enough

LEADER: *Dayenu* means it would have been enough. The song answers the question, "For how many favors do we owe praise to God?" The answer is "unending." If the LORD had done any one of the mighty acts of the Exodus, that would have been enough for us, or in Hebrew, "Dayenu." But the LORD continually saves and provides!

> ☞ **The Leader reads the verse, and the participants respond by singing or saying, "Dayenu!"**

If He had only brought us out of Egypt,
but had not punished the Egyptians – Dayenu!

If He had only punished the Egyptians,
but had not destroyed their gods – Dayenu!

If He had only destroyed their gods,
but had not slain their firstborn – Dayenu!

If He had only slain their firstborn,
but had not given us their wealth – Dayenu!

If He had only given us their wealth,
but had not divided the sea for us – Dayenu!

If He had only divided the sea for us,
but had not led us through on dry ground – Dayenu!

If He had only drowned our oppressors,
but had not provided for us in the desert for forty years – Dayenu!

If He had only fed us with manna,
but had not given us the Sabbath – Dayenu!

24

If He had only given us the Sabbath,
but had not brought us to Mt. Sinai – Dayenu!

If He had only brought us to Mt Sinai,
but had not given us the Torah – Dayenu!

If He had only given us the Torah,
but had not brought us into the Land of Israel – Dayenu!

If He had only brought us into the Land of Israel,
but had not built us the Temple – Dayenu!

INSTRUCTOR: Believers in Jesus can add:

Had Messiah only come to show us God's love and glory,
but had not died for our sins – Dayenu!

Had Messiah only died for our sins,
but was not raised to give us eternal life – Dayenu!

Had Messiah only been raised to give us eternal life,
but had not sent us His Spirit – Dayenu!

Had Messiah only sent us His Spirit,
but was not returning to bring us into eternal fellowship
with the Father – Dayenu!

ALL: BUT HE IS COMING!

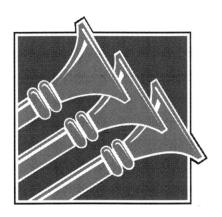

The Table of Jesus

INSTRUCTOR: Many years passed since Israel celebrated Passover in Egypt. With God's mighty signs and wonders, they began their journey to the Promised Land. Continuously God protected and provided for them: He fed them manna from heaven, their clothes never wore out, and their feet never swelled. All He asked was that they would love, trust, and obey Him.

But they did not; they could not. Over and over God tested them. Over and over they failed. Rather than love, they murmured against Him. Rather than trust, they depended on their own strength. Rather than obey, they rebelled. They were freed from Egypt but were still in bondage to sin.

 Finally God gave them His law, the Covenant of Moses, written on stone. The law defined and described what God expected of them as His people.

Israel promised that in return they would love and worship Him; but they broke their promise. Yet God was as patient with them as He is with us. Nevertheless for forty years, until the generation that had come out of Egypt had died and a new generation was born, Israel journeyed in the desert.

Eventually Moses died and Joshua became the leader. Finally God said that Israel was ready; but first God instructed Joshua to celebrate the Passover.

But even after they entered the Land and built the Temple, Israel continued to sin. The people constantly had to bring sacrifices to the Temple to make atonement because God's law said, "For the life of the flesh is in the blood, and I have given it to you upon the altar to make atonement for your souls; for it is the blood that makes atonement for the soul."

26

From the very beginning, God planned another, a better way. God promised that He would be the atonement for sin, that He would provide **Himself** as their atonement. He would BECOME their Savior. And He did. The root of the Hebrew word for *salvation* is [*yasha*], from which we get *Yeshua*, the Hebrew name for Jesus.

INSTRUCTOR: At this point we are going to change our focus. Let's go to Jerusalem around the year 32.

Jerusalem is filled with pilgrims who have come to celebrate the Passover in accordance with God's command in Deuteronomy 16:16. Over 260,000 lambs would be slain—and that's not one lamb per person but per family unit! The historian Josephus estimates that over 2,600,000 people filled the City of the Great King. Of course many hoped that the Rabbi from Nazareth would be there. Jerusalem was alive with activity: the priests plotted, the people prepared, and the disciples pondered.

Already there had been a month of preparation as homes had been cleansed of all leaven. This Passover might be the first time many pilgrims would have the chance to go through purification rites. So that none of the pilgrims would be rendered unclean by coming into contact with a dead body, the sepulchers had been whitewashed. It was against this outward form of holiness that Jesus had railed (Matthew 23:27; John 11:55).

The time of Passover had come. The sound of singing could be heard throughout the hills surrounding Jerusalem as the pilgrims sang the Great Hallel, Psalms 113–118.

HALLEL: PSALMS 113–115

INSTRUCTOR: *Hallel* is the Hebrew word meaning *praise.* The word *hallelujah,* which combines *Hallel* and *Yah* (short for Yahweh), means "praise YHWH." We have been created to praise and worship God.

Since the Hallel Psalms are read at Passover, Jesus and the disciples would probably have sung them at their Passover celebrations as they were growing up.

RESPONSIVE READING

☞ Leader reads the bold text and ALL respond, reading the italics text.

Praise the LORD! Praise, O servants of the LORD, praise the name of the LORD!

Blessed be the name of the LORD from this time forth forevermore.

Who is like the LORD our God, Who dwells on high, Who humbles Himself to behold the things that are in the heavens and the earth?

He raises the poor out of the dust and lifts the needy from the ash heap;

That He may seat him with princes—with the princes of his people. He grants the barren woman a home, like a joyful mother of children.

ALL: *Praise the LORD!*

*When Israel went out of Egypt, the house of Jacob from a people of strange language,

*Judah became His sanctuary, and Israel His dominion.

*Tremble, O earth, at the presence of the LORD, at the presence of the God of Jacob.

Not to us, O Lord, not to us but to Your name give glory, because of Your mercy and because of Your truth.

Why should the nations say, "Where now is their God?" But our God is in heaven; He does whatever He pleases.

Their idols are silver and gold, the work of men's hands. Those who make them are like them.

You who fear the Lord, trust in the Lord; He is their help and their shield.

The Lord has been mindful of us; He will bless us.

We will bless the Lord from this time forth and forevermore.

ALL: Praise the Lord!

Bgida: The Betrayal

INSTRUCTOR: Now let's join Jesus and the disciples at their table.

Remember how only the master washed his hands before eating the matzah? Now it was time for Jesus to wash His hands. But wait, what is happening? Jesus isn't washing His hands. Look!

"He got up from the meal, took off His outer clothing, and wrapped a towel around His waist. After that, He poured water into a basin and began to wash His disciples' feet, drying them with the towel that was wrapped around Him."

LEADER: He came to Simon Peter, who said to him, "Lord, are you washing my feet?"

READER #1: Jesus replied, "What I am doing you do not understand now, but you will know after this."

Last Supper Seating Chart: redrawn from book V, p. 494 of *The Life and Times of Jesus the Messiah* by Alfred Edersheim (1971).

29

READER #2: "NO!" Peter said, "You shall never wash my feet!"

READER #1: Jesus answered, "If I do not wash you, you have no part with Me."

READER #2: "Then, Lord," Simon Peter replied, "not my feet only, but also my hands and my head!"

READER #1: Jesus said to him, "He who is bathed needs only to wash his feet, but is completely clean . . . but not all of you. I know whom I have chosen; but that the Scripture may be fulfilled, 'He who eats bread with Me has lifted up his heel against Me.'"

INSTRUCTOR: If you listen carefully, you can figure out who was sitting where:

- The disciple whom Jesus loved was reclining next to Him.
- Simon Peter motioned to this disciple and said, "Ask Him which one."
- Leaning back against Jesus, he asked Him, "Lord who is it?"

People didn't use chairs back then; they reclined on their left sides. So John had to be sitting on the right side (or in front) of Jesus so that he could lie back on Jesus' breast. Probably Simon Peter was across the table from John. Listen again and you'll know where Judas sat.

Jesus answered, "It is he to whom I shall give a piece of bread when I have dipped it." And having dipped the bread, He gave it to Judas Iscariot, the son of Simon."

Judas was sitting on Jesus' left, or above Him. One scholar tells us that Judas was in the place of honor. So whose feet did Jesus wash first? JUDAS! Remember, Jesus knew that it was Judas who was going to betray Him yet He washed Judas' feet first. He could love even His enemy.

ALL: Jesus knew that the Father had put all things under His power, and that He had come from God and was returning to God.

INSTRUCTOR: Remember how we dipped the matzah into the bitter herbs? Now Jesus dipped the matzah into the bitter herbs and handed it to Judas. With the taste of bitterness still in his mouth, Judas got up, left the room, and went to the Pharisees to betray Jesus.

Shulchan Orech: **Dinner**

☞ Before resuming the service, clear all the tables except for the wine and wine glasses.

~ Resume service ~

INSTRUCTOR: Try to imagine what was going on in the minds and hearts of the men around that table.

What was Jesus thinking? What was He feeling? This was His last dinner with His disciples. He had so much to tell them.

The disciples were confused. Jesus and the disciples had celebrated Passover with their families all their lives. They knew the traditions and the rituals that had developed. But this night was different. Jesus was changing some of the rituals. But the real confusion was because of what He was saying. His words didn't make sense. They had seen the miracles He had done. They had heard the shouts of adoration of the people as they had walked with Him into Jerusalem just four days before. Yet, again, He was talking about leaving them.

Jesus knew the disciples were confused; He knew they had been blinded by their own misunderstanding of freedom. He had warned them about this trip to Jerusalem, but they had forgotten the words of their own prophets: "We are going up to Jerusalem, and all things that are written by the prophets concerning the Son of Man will be accomplished. For He will be delivered to the Gentiles and will be mocked and insulted and spit upon. They will scourge Him and put Him to death."

Neveim: The Prophets Speak

> ⤳ Everyone closes their eyes and listens to this dramatic reading from Psalm 22 and Isaiah 53.

Adult #1: He shall grow up before Him like a tender plant, and as a root out of dry ground. He has no form or comeliness; and when we see Him, there is no beauty that we should desire Him.

He is despised and rejected by men, a Man of sorrows and acquainted with grief. And we hid, as it were, our faces from Him; He was despised, and we did not esteem Him.

Adult #2: My God, My God, why have You forsaken Me? Why are You so far from helping Me, and from the words of My groaning? O my God, I cry in the daytime, but You do not hear.

But You are holy, enthroned in the praises of Israel. Our fathers trusted in You; they trusted, and You delivered them.

But I am a worm, and no man; a reproach of men, and despised by the people. All those who see Me ridicule Me; they shoot out the lip, they shake the head, saying, "He trusted in the Lord, let Him rescue Him."

Adult #1: All we like sheep have gone astray; we have turned, every one, to his own way; and the Lord has laid on Him the iniquity of us all.

Adult #2: Be not far from Me, for trouble is near; for there is none to help.

Adult #1: Surely He has borne our griefs and carried our sorrows; yet we esteemed Him stricken, smitten by God, and afflicted. But He was wounded for our transgressions; He was bruised for our iniquities.

Adult #2: I am poured out like water, and all My bones are out of joint. My heart is like wax; it has melted within Me.

Adult #1: He was oppressed and He was afflicted, yet He opened not His mouth; He was led as a lamb to the slaughter.

Adult #2: They pierced My hands and My feet; I can count all My bones. They look at Me and stare at Me. They divide My garments among them, and for My clothing they cast lots.

Adult #1: And they made His grave with the wicked— but with the rich at His death, because He had done no violence, nor was any deceit in His mouth.

Adult #2: O LORD do not be far from Me; O My Strength, hasten to help Me. Deliver my life from the power of the dog.

Adult #1: Yet it pleased the LORD to bruise Him; He has put Him to grief. When you make His soul an offering for sin, He shall see is seed, He shall prolong His days and the pleasure of the LORD will prosper in His hand. He shall see the labor of His soul, and be satisfied. By His knowledge My righteous Servant shall justify many for He shall bear their iniquities.

Adult #3: You who fear the LORD, praise Him! For He has not despised or abhorred the affliction of the afflicted; nor has He hidden His face from Him; but when He cried to Him, He heard.

The poor will eat and be satisfied; those who seek Him will praise the LORD. All the ends of the world shall remember and turn to the LORD. And all the families of the nations shall worship before You. A posterity shall serve Him. It will be recounted of the LORD to the next generation. They will come and declare His righteousness to a people who will be born.

Adult #1: *He has done it!* He bore the sin of many and made intercession for the transgressors. The chastisement for our peace was upon Him and by His stripes we are healed.

☛ **Sing a song of worship that focuses on the cross.**

INSTRUCTOR: Jesus knew it was almost time for Him to go to the cross and be crucified. He had so much to say to the disciples and to us. John records what Jesus said that night.

(For shorter service, skip to page 35.)

*INSTRUCTOR: Let's listen.

*READER #1: "Little children, I shall be with you a little while longer. You will seek Me; where I am going you cannot come, so now I say to you, 'Let not your heart be troubled; you believe in God, believe also in Me.'

*READER #2: "In My Father's house are many mansions; if it were not so I would have told you. I go to prepare a place for you. I will come again and receive you to Myself; that where I am there you may be also.

*READER #3: "I am the way, the truth, and the life. No one comes to the Father except through Me.

*READER #4 "Believe Me that I am in the Father and the Father in Me, or else believe Me for the sake of the works themselves.

*MEN: "I am the vine, you are the branches. He who abides in Me, and I in him, bears much fruit; for without Me you can do nothing.

*WOMEN: "If you abide in Me, and My words abide in you, you will ask what you desire and it shall be done for you.

*READER #5: "By this My Father is glorified, that you bear much fruit; so you will be My disciples. You did not chose Me, but I chose you and appointed you that you should go and bear fruit and that your fruit should remain.

*READER #6: "I will not leave you orphans; I will come to you. If anyone loves Me, My Father will love him and we will come to him and make our home with Him.

*READER #7: "The Helper, the Holy Spirit, whom the Father will send in My name, He will teach you all things, and bring to your remembrance all things that I said to you.

*ALL: "He is the Holy Spirit who will guide you into all truth.

*READER #8: "If the world hates you, you know that it hated Me before it hated you. Because you are not of the world, but I chose you out of the world, therefore the world hates you. If they persecuted Me, they will also persecute you.

*READER #9: "As the Father loved Me, I also have loved you; abide in My love.

*READER #10: "These things I have spoken to you, that you should not be made to stumble.

*LEADER: "No longer do I call you servants, for a servant does not know what his master is doing; but I have called you friends.

*MEN: "A new command I give you, love one another. By this all will know that you are My disciples.

*WOMEN: "I have told you these things so that in Me you may have peace.

*ALL: "Peace I leave with you, My peace I give to you. I do not give as the world gives.

*WOMEN: "In the world you will have trouble.

*MEN: "But take heart.

*ALL: "I have overcome the world."

~ Resume service ~

INSTRUCTOR: Before we can continue, we need to find that broken and hidden piece of matzha, which is called the *afikoman* meaning *that which comes after.* Like so many of the traditions that have been added to the Passover celebration, this one gives us a vivid picture of our redemption in Yeshua, Jesus.

> ☞ All the children look for the afikoman with the en-
> couragement of the people at their tables, calling out
> "hot/cold" as they get nearer or farther. Anyone can
> choose to find the afikoman from the Leader's table.
> The afikoman must be held for ransom until a negoti-
> ated "deal" can be made between the finder and the
> Leader or the host at each table.

INSTRUCTOR: What we've just experienced shows us the process of ransom, or redemption; that is, receiving the transfer of ownership from one
to another through payment of a price or an equivalent substitute. Several
Hebrew words are used for ransom or redemption. Often the Hebrew root
[*pada*] is used. This word can be applied to Jesus as He paid the ransom
to redeem us back from Satan. The purchase price was His blood.

THE TABLE OF JESUS (cont'd)

TZAFUN: THE BROKEN BODY

> ☞ The Instructor takes the matzah and reads:

INSTRUCTOR: And as they were eating, Jesus took the unleavened bread.
Perhaps He blessed it with the same blessing that Moses might have
used.

LEADER: *Baruch atah Adonai, Elohaynu Melech ha'olam, hamotzee
lechhem min haaretz.*

ALL: Blessed are You, O LORD our God, who brings forth bread from the earth and manna from heaven.

INSTRUCTOR: And then He said, "Take, eat, this is My body broken for you. Do this in remembrance of Me. I am the Bread of Life. Eating of this bread will give you eternal life."

> Instructor extends the invitation for salvation on page 46.

> The table hosts break the matzah and distribute.

We eat this bread in memory and gratitude of the broken body of our Messiah, Jesus.

> All eat.

KOS YESHUOT: THE CUP OF SALVATION

LEADER: We come to the third cup that is called by two names, the Cup of Redemption and the Cup of Salvation. It is based on God's third promise:

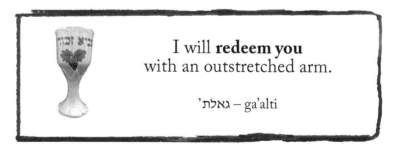

I will **redeem you**
with an outstretched arm.

גאלתי – ga'alti

INSTRUCTOR: There is another Hebrew word for *redeem* or *redemption.* When the ransom is paid by the closest relative, called the kinsman redeemer, the Hebrew root used is [*ga'al*]. From this root we get the word *goel*. This word can also be applied to Jesus; He is our *goel* because He is our closest relative.

The second name, the Cup of Salvation comes from Psalm 116 that is sung at this time. As we have seen, the Hebrew word for salvation, *yeshua*, comes from the Hebrew root [*yasha*], which literally means *having room to breathe* or *released from bondage or constriction*. This is such a wonderful picture of our redemption and salvation.

Let us sing this liturgy written by David and sung by Yeshua/Jesus:

LEADER: I love the LORD, because He has heard my voice and my supplications.

MEN: Because He has inclined His ear to me, therefore I will call upon Him as long as I live.

WOMEN: I called upon the name of the LORD: "O LORD, I implore You, deliver my soul!"

READER #1: Gracious is the LORD, and righteous; yes, our God is merciful. I was brought low, and He saved me.

ALL: The LORD has been good to me.

READER #2: What shall I render to the LORD for all His benefits toward me?

ALL: I will take up the *cup of salvation*, and call upon the name of the LORD.

INSTRUCTOR: The Hebrew actually reads, "cup of salvations." In other words, the cup that Jesus, Yeshua, offers is filled with many salvations. We are reconciled to God by His death, but much more, we are saved by His life!

Then Yeshua/Jesus took the cup, and gave thanks:

Barruch atah Adonai, Elohaynu Melech ha'olam, boray p'ree hagafen.

All: Blessed are You, O LORD our God, King of the Universe, who makes the fruit of the vine.

INSTRUCTOR: And He gave the cup to them, saying, "Drink from it, all of you. For this is My blood of the new covenant, which is shed for many for the remission of sins."

☞ **Instructor extends the invitation for recommitment on page 47.**

We drink this cup in celebration and memory of the shed blood of Yeshua, our Passover Lamb.

☞ **All drink.**

HALLEL: PSALMS **116–118**

READER #1: Oh, give thanks to the LORD, for He is good! For His mercy endures forever.

READER #2: I called on the LORD in distress; the LORD answered me and set me in a broad place.

READER #3: The LORD is on my side; I will not fear. What can man do to me?

READER #4: It is better to trust in the LORD than to put confidence in man.

LEADER: The voice of rejoicing and salvation is in the tents of the righteous; the right hand of the LORD does valiantly. The right hand of the LORD is exalted; the right hand of the LORD does valiantly.

READER #5: I shall not die, but live, and declare the works of the LORD. The LORD has chastened me severely, but He has not given me over to death.

READER #6: The stone which the builders rejected has become the chief cornerstone. This was the LORD's doing; it is marvelous in our eyes.

MEN: This is the day the LORD has made; we will rejoice and be glad in it.

WOMEN: You are my God, and I will praise You.

ALL: Oh, give thanks to the LORD, for He is good! For His mercy endures forever.

INSTRUCTOR: At this point in the Seder, it was customary to take the fourth cup of wine, finish singing the *Hallel*, and declare the service completed. But Jesus did not drink this fourth cup; there was another cup from which He had to drink—the cup of God's wrath. Instead, He took this fourth cup and said, "I say to you, I will not drink of the fruit of the vine until the kingdom of God comes." Although the Passover ritual was not finished, Jesus and his disciples sang a hymn and went to the Mount of Olives to the place called *Gethsemane*, which means *olive press*. While He prayed and Peter and John slept, Judas led a band of Roman soldiers to arrest Jesus. During the rest of the night and the next day, Jesus was on trial before Herod and then Pilate. Pilate declared him innocent, but the religious leaders cried out, "Crucify Him!"

So Pilate ordered Jesus beaten with a lead-tipped whip, and turned Him over to the Roman soldiers to be crucified.

Jesus was treated horribly. Some of the governor's soldiers took Him into their headquarters and called out the entire regiment. They stripped Him and put a scarlet robe on Him. They wove thorn branches into a crown and put it on His head, and they placed a reed stick in His right hand as a scepter. Then they knelt before Him in mockery and taunted, "Hail! King of the Jews!" And they spit on Him and grabbed the stick and struck Him on the head with it. When they were finally tired of mocking Him, they took off the robe and put His own clothes on Him again. Then they led Him away to be crucified.

Jesus never argued or fought back. He went through all of this because of love. Love for you. Love for the world. Isaiah wrote: "He was wounded for our transgressions, He was bruised for our iniquities; the chastisement for our peace was upon Him, and by His stripes we are healed."

The Roman soldiers found a man of Cyrene and compelled him to carry Jesus' cross to a place called *Golgotha* that means *the place of the skull*. There they crucified Jesus. While He hung on the cross, they offered Him wine mixed with gall to drink. But when He tasted it, He would not drink. Perhaps He was waiting to share the fourth and final Passover cup with us.

*In God's perfect timing and on *His* calendar, on the very day that the blood of the Passover lamb protected Israel in Egypt on that first Passover, Jesus the ultimate Passover Lamb died on a cross in Jerusalem.

*The reason we celebrate Passover in this new way is to remember and celebrate God's love and what Jesus did on that day. Real freedom for Israel and for the world only comes through the blood of Jesus. In Jesus we can find freedom from the slavery and bondage of our sins, our sorrows, and our sicknesses.

Jesus was crucified on Passover and buried on the Feast of Unleavened Bread, separating our sins from us as far as the east is from the west. But then, on the third day, on the Feast of Firstfruits, Jesus rose from the dead. That's why He is called "the firstfruits from the dead." He is alive! Jesus conquered death!

Of course that's not the end of the story either. There will be another table. Remember Jesus said to the disciples, "I tell you now that I won't eat this meal again until it is fulfilled in the Kingdom of God." Forty days after He rose from His grave, Jesus went back to heaven. There He is waiting, planning, and preparing for another table and another cup of wine to celebrate His marriage—the Marriage Supper of the Passover Lamb!

🔖 **Sing a song that focuses on heaven.**

During the song, table hostesses place simple wedding decorations on the table.

The Marriage Supper

INSTRUCTOR: Now we are ready, by faith, to take our seats at the last table in the New Jerusalem. Our journeys are finished. Our battles are over, and the victory is won. We are free. We are whole. All our hopes and dreams have been fulfilled.

Every knee is bowing and every tongue is confessing that Messiah Jesus is Lord, and the new heavens and new earth are filled with the knowledge of His glory.

The sun and the moon are gone because Jesus is the light. There is no more death. There is no more crying. There are no more tears. There is no more sickness, for the old order of things has passed away.

Listen to the loud voice of a great multitude in heaven saying:

ALL: "Alleluia! Salvation and glory and honor and power to the Lord our God."

MEN: Praise our God all you His servants and those who fear Him, both small and great.

LEADER: The sound of many waters as the sound of mighty thunderings is saying:

WOMEN: "Alleluia! For the Lord God Omnipotent reigns!"

INSTRUCTOR: Let us be glad and rejoice and give Him glory, for the marriage of the Lamb has come, and His wife has made herself ready.

Kos Lakachti: The Cup of the Kingdom

INSTRUCTOR: As we look forward in faith to that table, we prepare to drink the fourth cup, called the Cup of the Kingdom or the Cup of Praise. Sometimes it's even called the Cup of Restoration. It is based on the fourth promise of God:

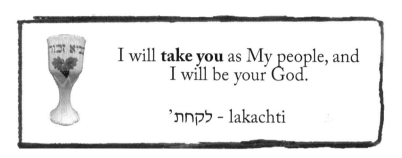

I will **take you** as My people, and I will be your God.

לקחתי - lakachti

INSTRUCTOR: The invitation was given and you accepted.

*To you who are thirsty, I will give to drink without cost from the spring of the River of Life. You who have overcome have inherited all of this, and I am your God and you are My sons and daughters. But the cowardly, the unbelieving, the vile, the murderers, the sexually immoral, those who practice magic arts, the idolaters and all liars—their place will be in the fiery lake of burning sulphur.

To you it has been granted to be arrayed in fine linen clean and bright, for the fine linen is the righteous acts of the saints. Take your seat at the table. The banner over you is love. See the white stone at your place with your new name that no one else will know. But you will know. You might know already!

ALL: Praise the Lord! Salvation and glory and power belong to our God.

LEADER: Look! There is the throne and the One sitting on it has the appearance of jasper and carnelian. A rainbow resembling an emerald encircles the throne.

MEN: Surrounding it are the thrones of twenty-four elders.

WOMEN: They are dressed in white and have crowns of gold on their heads.

LEADER: There are four living creatures, each having six wings, full of eyes around and within. And they do not rest day or night, saying:

ALL: "Holy, holy, holy, the Lord God the Almighty, who was and is and is to come."

LEADER: The twenty-four elders and four living beings fall down and worship God, who is sitting on the throne, and cry out, "Amen! Praise the LORD!"

INSTRUCTOR: And in the center of the throne, encircled by the four living creatures and the elders, is the Lion of Judah looking like a lamb that was slain! Look carefully and you can see the nail prints in His hands. They are shining like silver, like the silver pieces Judas received to betray Him or the cost of redeeming the firstborn. But wait, look again. The wounds spell out YOUR NAME! From before the foundation of the world, your name was written on His hands!

MEN: You are worthy because You were slain and with Your blood You have purchased men for God.

WOMEN: From every tribe and language and people and nation.

ALL: Worthy is the Lamb who was slain to receive power and riches and wisdom, strength and honor, glory and blessing!

LEADER: Let us take the Cup of the Kingdom and say, "Blessing and honor and glory and power be to Him who sits on the throne, and to the Lamb, forever and ever."

☞ **All drink.**

ALL: Amen! Praise and glory and wisdom and thanks and honor and power and strength be to our God forever and ever. AMEN!

☞ **Worship and praise.**

LEADER: *TETALASTI!*

Our celebration is now concluded, but there is a traditional end to the Passover service, a prayer that the Jewish people have been praying for thousands of years. We can say with them:

ALL: NEXT YEAR IN THE NEW JERUSALEM!

Invitations

PRAYER FOR SALVATION

Beloved of God, Jesus is extending His nail-pierced hand to you to deliver you from the bondage of sin, sorrow, and sickness. He carried all your past, your present, and your future on His back to the Cross. It is by God's grace through your faith in His sacrifice that will bring you into an eternal, personal, and intimate relationship with God.

Four things are important for you to understand.

1. You were born and remain in bondage to sin. God's standards are higher than man's. You must be ready to confess and repent from your sin.

2. Jesus is the only way to salvation, to a personal relationship with God.

3. When you enter into the New Covenant, you are filled with the Holy Spirit and your life is in God's hands. To grow in His grace, wisdom, and become the person you were created to be, you must completely trust His love and surrender to His will. This is a continual process.

4. Your name will be written in the Lamb's Book of Life for all eternity and nothing will separate you from His love.

Father in Heaven, I confess that I have lived a life of sin and I ask you now to forgive me of all my sins: those I remember and those I've forgotten. Forgive my sin of actions and of thoughts. I believe that Jesus is the Passover Lamb whose blood will protect me from Your wrath and punishment of my sin. I believe that He is the only way to salvation and I give you my heart and my life. Thank You for Your forgiveness and Your Holy Spirit. With Your help I will follow and obey You all the days of my life. Thank You for Your love and Your promise to never leave or forsake me. In Jesus name I pray.

PRAYER FOR RECOMMITMENT

My Father, thank You for Your faithful love. You were faithful when I was not. I confess that I have wandered far away from You—sometimes by my thoughts, and sometimes by my actions. I have tried to be in control of my life and it hasn't worked! You are God and I am not. I need You, Father. I don't want to live another minute without Your sweet Presence. Please forgive me of my sins and even my neglect when I've put people or things ahead of You. Wash me by the blood of the Passover Lamb. Help me, Holy Spirit, to know the Father's love. Fill me again with the sense of Your peace, Your love, and Your joy. Jesus, I give you my hand, my heart, and my life. Thank You for Your abundant forgiveness and grace. I am Yours and You are mine. In Your name, Jesus, I pray.

Supplemental Notes

The Plagues

God designed the first nine plagues to humiliate the Egyptian gods, proving their impotence and His omnipotence.[1]

- Blood: The River Nile was worshipped as Hapi, the giver of life.

- Frogs: Hektor was the male representation of the goddess Hathor.

- Lice: Isis, the goddess of magic and healing, was the wife of Isiris.

- Flies: Hathor, goddess of music, dance, fertility, and foreign lands, was commonly depicted as a cow goddess with head horns in which was set a sun disc.[2]

- Disease and boils: Ptah (or Apis) was the bull god of Memphis.

- Locusts: Serapis was the god of protection against locusts.

- Hail and darkness: Ra, the sun god, was the supreme of all Egyptian gods.

There was a distinct pattern of the first nine plagues: triplets increasing in severity. Each triplet began with Moses meeting Pharaoh at the water to warn him of impending danger. The second plague in each triplet came with a warning but without God specifying the time or place. There was no warning for the third of each triplet.

SEARCHING FOR LEAVEN

Seven days you shall eat unleavened bread. On the first day you shall remove leaven from your houses. For whoever eats leavened bread from the first day until the seventh day, that person shall be cut off from Israel. Exodus 12:15

There is a traditional ritual for searching and cleansing the house of leaven among observant Jewish families. This ritual is based on an interpretation of Scripture. The interpretation says, "I will search Jerusalem with lamps and punish those who are complacent."

The Jewish Encyclopedia explains the ritual:

> Many days before Passover the pious Jewish housewife commences her house-cleaning for the festival. On the eve of the fourteenth of Nissan, although most Jewish houses are then thoroughly free from all leaven, the master of the house proceeds with the ceremony of searching for leaven. Pieces of bread are placed in conspicuous places which cannot be overlooked, and with a wax candle in his hand the master of the house begins the search, after pronouncing the following blessing: "Blessed art thou O Lord our God, King of the Universe who has sanctified us by Your commandments and commands us concerning the removal of leavened bread."

> After he has searched all the rooms and has collected all the morsels of leaven in a wooden spoon, he carefully ties them up in a rag and stores them away in a place which cannot be reached by rats, pronouncing the following formula in Aramaic or in any language which he understands best: "Let all leaven that is in my premises which I have not seen and which I have not removed be as of no avail and be as the dust of the ground." On the next morning leaven may be eaten only until the fourth hour of the day; and soon after that time all the remaining leaven is carefully collected and burned, when the master of the house repeats the formula, with a few alterations, which he recited on the previous evening (Orah Hayyim, 431-437).

> The chief purpose of the formal search is to give a religiolegal sanction to the actions of the housewife. [3]

Passover demands much preparation throughout Jewish communities, especially in Israel. Any establishment that handles food must go through a major overhaul. Any dish or machine that has touched food deemed to be leaven must be replaced if it is to be used during the holiday. Most restaurants simply close their doors and wait.

In supermarkets and grocery stores, all leavened products are gathered together and hidden behind a sheet. Everyone must take precautions and preparations, even if they do not adhere to the stringent rules of leaven given by the rabbis. I was astounded, when I went to get some grated Parmesan cheese at a time close to Passover, that the grater had been turned off. I never knew until then that cheese could be considered leaven. We can now better understand the implications of Paul's exhortation to search oneself for leaven before eating the Passover! (Read more at www.jewishencyclopedia.com)

Ancient Jewish Wedding Customs

The third and fourth cups of the Seder reflect ancient Jewish wedding customs. Take time to look up the referenced Scripture passages and you will gain a new understanding and appreciation of Communion.

The entire marriage process had two major components: the *kiddushin* which means *betrothal;* and the *huppa* meaning *canopy, room,* or *covering.* The betrothal was based on the acceptance of the *ketuba,* which was the marriage contract. The *huppa* was the actual consummation of the marriage.

Choosing the bride was the father's responsibility. He generally sent a trusted servant to find a suitable bride, to meet her parents, and to negotiate terms (Gen 24:2-4; John 15:16). Once the potential bride was selected, the groom paid a visit to the bride and made three presentations to her and to her family.

First the groom presented the "bride price" to the bride's father. The price reflected the value the groom placed on the bride (1 Peter 1:18-19; Eph. 1:13-14). The groom and his father also give gifts to the bride (John 10:37, 14:27; Mat. 18:19-20).

Second, the groom offered the ketuba which defined his responsibilities to the bride: provision, care, and fulfillment of his duties as a husband (Ex. 6:7, 19:5; Jer. 31:31; Heb. 8:6-13). The ketuba was signed by two witnesses and given to the bride and her father.

Lastly the groom presented wine which was a symbol of joy and blood. The wine was a reminder of the past when God brought judgment upon Egypt, and it reflected the anticipated joy when the Messiah will bring peace and blessing. Traditionally the groom offered the wine by saying, "This represents my life's blood. If you drink it you will be mine. I am willing to lay my life down for you."

If the bride accepted the marriage proposal, the ketuba was signed and the cup of wine was shared. However, the groom did not drink, preferring to wait until the marriage was consummated and their joy was fulfilled. At that time, they would drink another cup together (Matt. 26:29; Mark 14:25; Luke 22:18).

The betrothal could last from one to three years during which time the couple remained separate. The couple was considered married although the marriage had not been consummated. The betrothal was a time of preparation. Under his father's guidance, the groom prepared the huppa and the couple's future home (John 14:2-3). The bride purified herself (2 Cor. 11:2; 2 Tim. 2:1; 1 Peter 1:15-16; Rev. 19:7), learned to be a wife and mother, and anticipated the return of her groom. Because she did not know when he would return, she kept a full oil lamp by her bedside (Matt. 25:1-13).

When the groom's father determined that all was ready, the groom returned (usually at night) with a shout and "abducted" his bride (1 Thess. 4:16-18, 5:2). The couple was adorned as a king and queen, even to the wearing of crowns (Ps. 45: 8-15; Isa. 61:10; Rev. 19:7-8). The friends of the bridegroom led the couple to the huppa where they sequestered themselves for seven days and consummated their marriage (Ex. 19:18; Isa. 4:4-6).

Finally the couple emerged to celebrate their joy with their friends and drink the Cup of the Kingdom!

Notes

1   Glashouwer, Willem, J.J., *Why Israel?* (Manassas, VA: Christians for Israel, 2001), 59.

2   "Hatho" available at http://en.wikipedia.org/wiki/Hathor.

3   "Leaven" available at www.jewishencyclopedia.com/view. jsp?artid=128&letter=L

Explanation of Terms

PASSOVER:

The Hebrew word for "pass over" [*pesach*] is better translated as "spring or leap over," yet it has the connotation of hovering over, as a bird hovers over its nest. Actually I prefer this meaning because of the picture it evokes. Whenever God saw the blood of the lamb upon a doorpost, He would hover over it, giving protection to those inside as the plague would "spring over."

ONE:

There are at least two Hebrew words translated as "one." Both have tremendous significance to the character of God.

Echad is a compound unity of separate entities. In English examples of compound unity words are: team, flock, herd, and class. *Echad* is used to describe God in the most important prayer of Judaism, the Shema (Deuteronomy 6:4): "Hear, O Israel: The LORD our God, the LORD is one!" *Echad* is also used to describe one day (night and day), one flesh (man and woman), and a cluster of grapes (Genesis 1:5, 2:24; Numbers 13:23).

The meaning of *yachid*[1] suggests "one and only, unique, or solitary." God used *yachid* to define which son Abraham was to sacrifice (Genesis 12:2): *Then He said, "Take now your son, your only son Isaac, whom you love, and go to the land of Moriah, and offer him there as a burnt offering."*

Certainly it would seem more than appropriate for God to use yachid to describe Himself. Truly He is solitary, unique, and the only God. But instead He used *echad* to reflect His triune nature.

I Am:

God gives His memorial name in the context of the Passover event, revealing His love, which constrained Him to rescue His people.

> Then the children of Israel groaned because of the bondage, and they cried out; and their cry came up to God because of the bondage. So God heard their groaning, and God remembered His covenant with Abraham, with Isaac, and with Jacob. And God looked upon the children of Israel, and God acknowledged them . . . "So I have come down to deliver them" . . . And God said to Moses, "I AM WHO I AM" . . . "This is My name forever, and this is My memorial to all generations." (Exodus 2:23–25, 3:8, 3:14-15)

Let's consider each of these verbs:[2]

God **heard** their groaning.

> Israel had no church building. There were no prayer meetings. Nor did the people have any written prayers they could recite. They weren't even praying. In fact, the Bible says that all they could do was groan. You've been in that place, haven't you, when you're too discouraged, too tired, too confused, or in too much pain to do anything else but groan? This passage says that God hears even the *groans* of His people.

God **remembered** His covenant.

> God does not forget. The only thing He chooses not to remember is our sin. He knew when it was time to fulfill the rest of His covenant promise to His people.

God **looked** upon the children.

> The Hebrew root [*ra'ah*] used here is beyond simply "to see or to look at . . . to inspect, perceive, consider."[3] In other words, it means to **really** see. If God knows the number of hairs on our heads, do you think there is anything in our lives He cannot or does not see?

God **acknowledged** them.

> Again we turn to the Hebrew for a better understanding of the word [*yada*]. It means "to know by experience, to recognize, admit, acknowledge, and confess." Further definitions include: "to consider, to know, be acquainted

with." God is thoroughly acquainted with our troubles and sorrows. Jesus was "a man of sorrows and acquainted with grief." He is able to sympathize with our weaknesses and suffering.

This verse is the key to God's name and why He chose Passover to reveal it. God came down to deliver Israel, redeem her, and rescue her out of bondage. This verse is also a picture of God's love for us. This love came to its fulfillment with Jesus, God the Son (Philippians 2:6-8).

These five actions of God—hearing, remembering, seeing, understanding, and coming down to deliver—are reflected in His name I AM, the One who is actively and intimately involved in our lives. He is the One who is uncreated, eternal, self-sufficient, and completely sufficient for all our needs.

REDEMPTION/DELIVERANCE (EXODUS 6:6-8):

I will *bring* you out.

> [*Yatza'*] means "to cause to go or come out, bring out, lead out." Who among us doesn't understand being under burdens? Israel's burdens were physical. She was in slavery to hard labor. Bondage and burdens come in many different forms: physical, emotional, relational, mental, financial, and of course the ultimate bondage, spiritual. Each of us has experienced at least one of these burdens or bondages. God still promises to "bring [us] out from under the burdens."

I will *rescue* you.

> [*Ntzl*] is the root that means "to snatch away, deliver, rescue, save, strip, and plunder." I love this Hebrew word that connotes strength and a violent ripping and tearing away. The Hebrew sounds like two Velcro strips being pulled apart. God went into Egypt and snatched Israel away quickly and violently. In the Hebrew translation of the New Testament, it is the same word translated as *delivered* in Colossians 1:13: "He has delivered us from the power of darkness and conveyed us into the kingdom of the Son of His love."

I will *redeem* you.

> [*Gā'al*] means "to redeem, act as kinsman-redeemer, avenge, revenge, ransom, do the part of a kinsman."4 This promise is the essence of the Passover story. In fact, it is the essence of the entirety of Scripture—God's redeeming

love. Redemption means "the paying of a ransom to achieve the transfer of ownership." The modern understanding of paying a ransom is of the weaker capitulating to the stronger. But this is not the biblical concept of redemption. God did not capitulate; Egypt could not hold Israel against God's will! No one and nothing can stand against the power of God.

Actually, there are two Hebrew words often translated as "rescue" or "redeem." One of them, [*pada*], is the *"actual ransom* payment." The other, [*gā'al*], focuses on the kinsman or closest relative, who pays the ransom. By using the word [*gā'al*] in this passage, God is promising that it will be He who ransoms Israel. God was giving us a picture of what was necessary to bring His people out of their bondage to sin.

SALVATION:

Yeshua [*yeshua*] is the Hebrew name translated as Jesus. It comes from the root [*yasha*], which means "to receive help, to be victorious, to accept help, also to save, help, to come to assist."[5]

Consider these verses: Genesis 42:24, Psalm 46:2, and Jeremiah 30:7. In each verse, the writer is facing severe trouble, anguish, distress, and affliction. The same root word is used in each of these verses: [*tsarar*], which means "to bind, be distressed, be cramped, be narrow, be scant."[6] We use English words like uptight, anxious, stressed, or bound up for the same idea.

Jesus saves, delivers, releases, and rescues us from trouble, distress, anxiety, anguish—whatever is pressing in upon us—in body, soul, or spirit. He is our salvation, bringing us out of our bondage and bringing us to a place where we can take a deep breath.

GRACE AND TRUTH:

Perhaps the worst misconception about God is that He changed. Most people would deny that they believe this idea, insisting that God is the same yesterday, today, and tomorrow. And yet, these same people will say that the God of the Old Testament is a God of Law and the God of the New Testament is the God of Grace.

This problem stems from a misinterpretation of John 1:17 relating to the comparison being made. The contrast is NOT between law versus grace and truth, but the *way* law, grace, and truth are mediated. At first, the mediation was by tablets of stone, which God gave by way of Moses. Then Jesus BECAME the New Covenant and the better mediator.

The God of Sinai revealed Himself to be grace [*hesed*] and truth [*emet*].[7] He is the same as the God of Calvary. Consistently throughout Scripture God is described as [*emet v'hesed*], which is grace *and* truth.[8]

Notes

1   www.blueletterbible.org/lang/lexicon/lexicon.cfm?Strongs=H3173&t=KJV.

2   Excerpted from: Lipis, Joan, *Celebrate Jesus! A Christian Perspective of the Feasts of the Lord,* (Keller, TX: Palm Tree Productions, 2009), 79–85.

3   www.blueletterbible.org/lang/lexicon/lexicon.cfm?Strongs=H7200&t=KJV.

4   *Theological Wordbook of the Old Testament,* (TWOT). (Chicago, IL: The Moody Bible Institute 1980), #300.

5   Koehler, L. & Baumgartner, W. (Eds.). *The Hebrew and Aramaic Lexicon of the Old Testament* (HALOT) [Electronic form. Leiden, Netherlands: Brill 2009] #8748.

6   Strong, J. *The Exhaustive Concordance of the Bible* [Electronic form]. Ontario: Woodside Bible Fellowship, 1996.

7   Exodus 34:6–7.

8   *Hesed* is often translated as "loving kindness" or "mercy." Consider these verses: Psalm 25:2; 36:5; 40:11; 85:10; 89:1; Proverbs 16:6; Micah 7:20.

Notes

Books and Media by Joan Lipis

Celebrate Jesus!: A Christian Perspective of the Biblical Feasts

Explore the significance of the feasts for your life and the community of the Kingdom.

Celebrate God's Love: Hanakkuh/Christmas, Fact and Fiction

Take a fresh look at two of our favorite holidays.

Celebrate Passover: The Three Tables Haggadah - A Messianic Celebration

Celebrate in Egypt with Moses, in Jerusalem with Jesus, and in the New Jerusalem at the Marriage Supper of the Lamb.

The Biblical Response to Israel - DVD

Discover the biblical purpose and plan for Israel.

To arrange a Passover Seder or other teaching, contact Joan at

novea@novea.org

To order these resources, visit

novea.org ~ celebratejesusthebook.com ~ Amazon.com